D1383558

find out about
ships
and boats

Written by
Sally Hewitt and Nicola Wright

Designed by
Chris Leishman

Illustrated by
Rachael O'Neill

Contents

Chrysalis Education

Afloat

All ships and boats, from giant supertankers to tiny rowing boats, have similar names for their different parts.

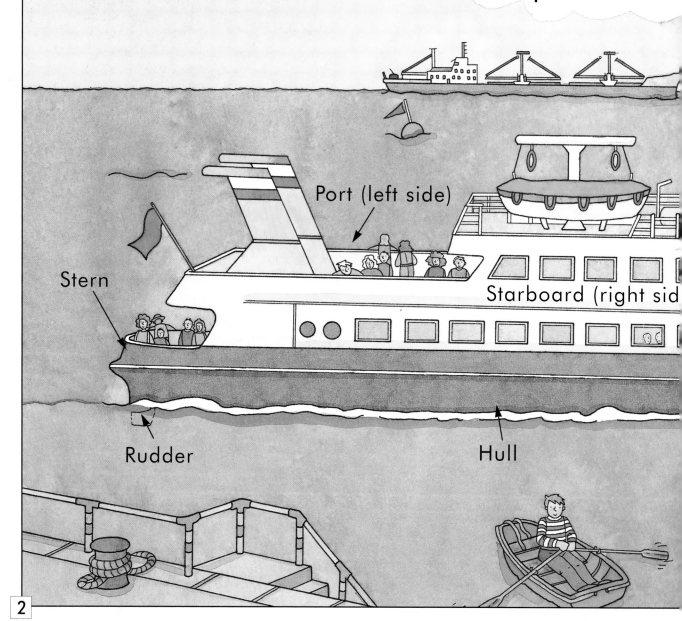

Port (left side)

Stern

Starboard (right sid

Rudder

Hull

Bow

Anchor

Engines are used to drive ships and boats of all sizes.

Sails Sailing boats move along when the wind fills their sails.

Oars and paddles Rowers pull oars and paddles through the water to move their boats along.

Ferries

Ferries carry passengers, cars, trucks, and sometimes even trains on short journeys from port to port.

Hovercraft
Hovercraft ride just above the waves on a cushion of air.

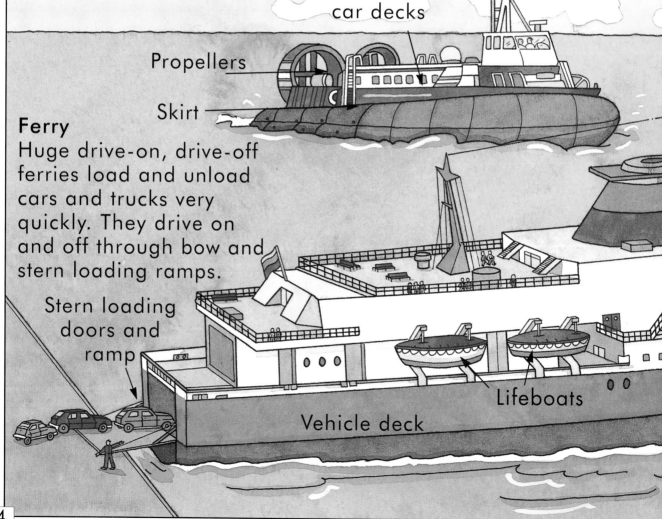

Passenger and car decks

Propellers

Skirt

Ferry
Huge drive-on, drive-off ferries load and unload cars and trucks very quickly. They drive on and off through bow and stern loading ramps.

Stern loading doors and ramp

Lifeboats

Vehicle deck

Hydrofoil
This ferry skims across the water on small, very strong wings called foils.

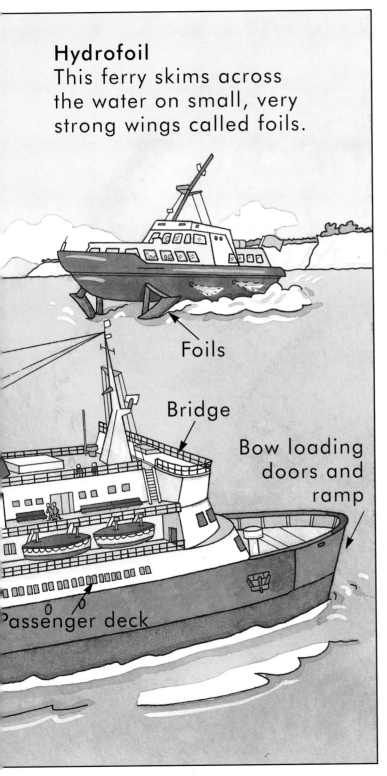

Foils

Bridge

Bow loading doors and ramp

Passenger deck

Skirt The hovercraft's skirt fills with air. It can ride on air over ground as well as on waves.

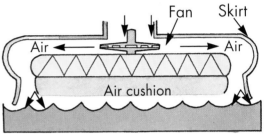

Fan   Skirt

Air ← → Air

Air cushion

Foils Foils are like aeroplane wings. Hydrofoils have to get up speed before they can "take off."

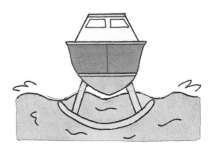

Fishing

Fishing at sea can be a dangerous job. Fishermen often risk their lives in storms and freezing weather.

Fish-factory ship
The catch is dropped onto a conveyor belt. Inside the ship the fish is cleaned, packed and frozen. It is often stored for weeks in a large refrigerated hold.

Winch

Ramp

Conveyer belt

Trawler
Trawlers are usually small.
The fish is packed in ice and
only keeps fresh for about
14 days.

Refrigerated
store

Bringing in the catch

A net called a **trawl**
is dragged through
the water.

A **winch** hauls the
trawl full
of fish
up the
stern
ramp.

The crew prepares
the fish in safety on
the **lower deck**.

Floating hotels

Cruise ships are big floating hotels. Passengers travel in comfort to interesting places all over the world. There is plenty to do on board.

Swimming pools

Shops

Dance Floor

Library

Cabins

Hospital

Theater

Lounge

Fun Fact

Passenger liners take about 3 days to cross the Atlantic. Concorde can fly from London to New York in under 4 hours!

Bridge The captain and officers control the ship from the bridge.

Stabilizers Small fins, called stabilizers, help to stop the ship rolling from side to side.

Propellers Powerful engines turn huge propellers which drive the ship through the water.

Cargo carriers

Some ships are specially built to carry enormous amounts of cargo. They can carry loads for long distances, from country to country.

Container ship
Containers arrive at the port on trucks and trains. High-speed lifting cranes then load them on to the container ship.

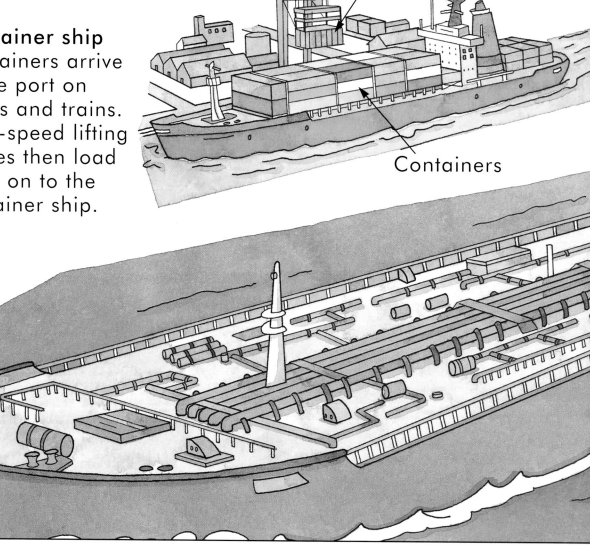

Moving crane

Containers

Supertanker

This supertanker carries over 500,000 tons of oil in rows of tanks in its hull.

Tank hatches

Supertankers are too big for most harbours. Oil is loaded and unloaded in deep water through **pipes** into

smaller tankers which carry the oil ashore.

Containers are big boxes filled with cargo that stack neatly together.

Fun Fact

Supertankers are so long that sometimes the crew ride bicycles to get from one end of the deck to the other!

Warships

Different kinds of warships are designed to fight on the water, underwater, or to help planes fight in the air.

Aircraft carrier
Fighter planes and helicopters take off and land on aircraft carriers.

Destroyer
Destroyers and cruisers armed with guns and missiles fight on the water.

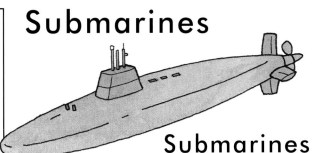

Submarines

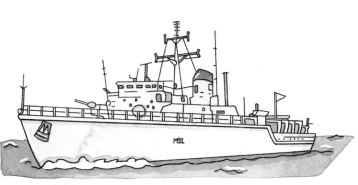

Minesweeper
Underwater explosives called mines are found and destroyed by minesweepers.

Submarines are ships that can travel underwater. They carry special missiles, called torpedoes, which can be fired underwater.

The **periscope** is the submarine's eye. It is a long tube with mirrors that reflect what is above the surface of the water.

Ships for special jobs

Dredgers are used to move mud off the seabed near to the shore so ships do not get stuck. They are also used to collect building materials such as rocks.

Fun Fact

Mud dumped out at sea is nearly always washed back in again!

Buckets

Chute

Barge

Icebreakers ride up onto the ice. The heavy bow breaks the ice. Then the extra-wide hull clears a wide path.

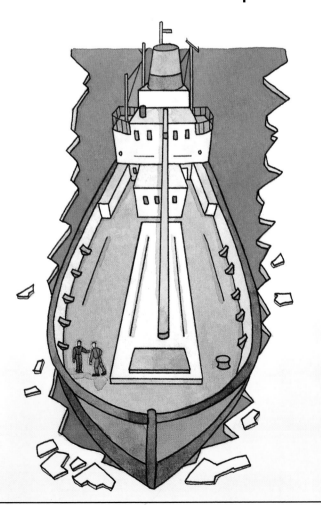

Special features

Dredger **buckets** move round on a ladder scooping up mud. It slides down chutes into barges and is dumped further out to sea.

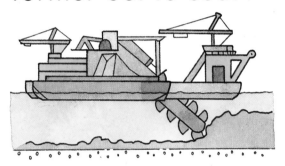

Some dredgers use pipes to suck up soft mud.

Sailing

Sailing ships, boats, and yachts catch the wind in their sails to move them along.

Sail

Forestay

Jib

Bow sprit

Shroud

Dinghy
One sail and a good wind is enough to speed this dinghy along.

Fun Fact

The first ships to sail right round the world took 3 years!

Yard

Mast

Brace

Gaff

Boom

Rudder

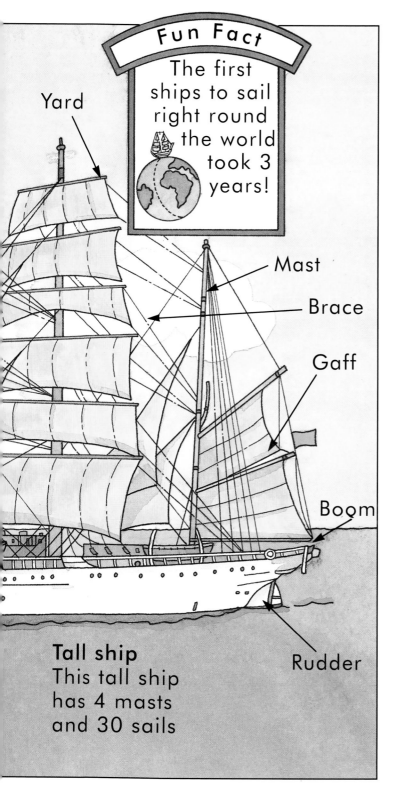

Tall ship
This tall ship has 4 masts and 30 sails

Sails

Sails are attached to a tall pole called a **mast**.

The sail is stretched out onto a **boom** which can swing round to catch the wind.

The crew control the sail with a rope called a **sheet**.

Speeding

Fast boats are built for racing, having fun, and also rescuing.

Racing boat
Racing boats have pointed bows and powerful engines.

Cruiser
You can eat, sleep, and live in comfort on board a cruiser.

Lifeboat
Lifeboats are specially designed to stay afloat in very rough seas.

Motorboat
A motorboat can tow a water-skier.

Outboard engines are fitted on the outside of a boat. They can be taken on and off.

Inboard engines are built into a boat.

Jet skis are like motorbikes on water.

Oars and paddles

Boats without engines or sails need human power to move them along.

Rowing boat

Racing shell
Racing shells can have eight oarsmen. The cox steers and shouts instructions to the crew.

Kayak
A kayak is a very light canoe.

Methods

One paddle
Canoeists hold one paddle with both hands. They push it into the water on either side of the canoe and pull back.

Two oars can be used on either side of a rowing boat.

One oar
Using one oar at the back of the boat is called sculling.

Finding the way

There are no roads and signposts at sea to help sailors. These are some of the things they use to help them find their way.

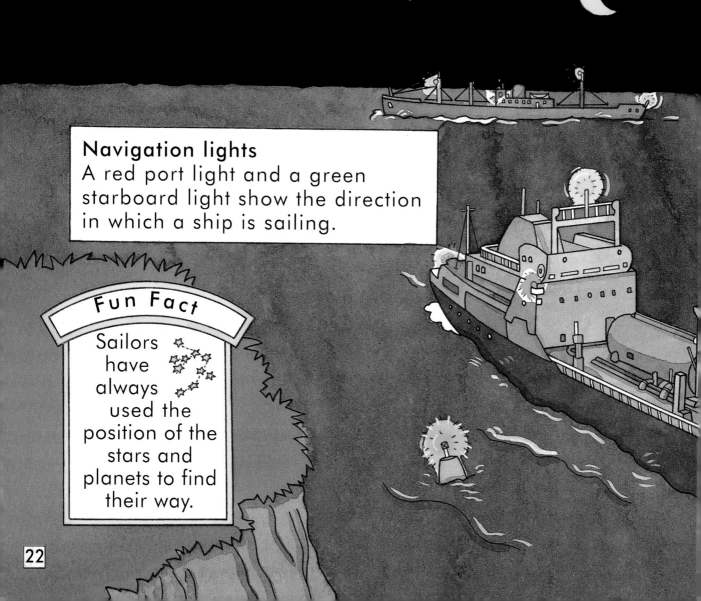

Navigation lights
A red port light and a green starboard light show the direction in which a ship is sailing.

Fun Fact
Sailors have always used the position of the stars and planets to find their way.

Satellite
Satellites send out signals that help ships to work out exactly where they are.

Lighthouse
Lighthouses mark harbor entrances and warn ships of dangerous rocks and tides.

Buoy
Floating marker buoys mark rocks and other possible dangers.

Radar shows where other ships and land are so ships can sail at night or in fog without colliding.

Charts are sea maps showing where dangerous rocks and sandbanks are.

A **compass** points to the North. Ships use them to work out which way to go.

Index

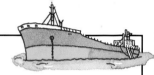

Edited by Nicola Wright and Dee Turner
Consultant: Robin Wright, M.M., M.A.
Design Manager: Kate Buxton
Printed in China

ISBN 1 84238 656 1

10 9 8 7 6 5 4 3 2 1

This edition first published in 2003 by
Chrysalis Children's Books
The Chrysalis Building, Bramley Rd, London W10 6SP

Copyright © Chrysalis Books PLC